BODY HORROR

DCSROSS

TELLING TALES OUT OF SCHOOL

I've told.
the truth
before
but it
got me
in trouble.

I don't
expect
this time
to be
any
different.

BETTER HALF

Lighting, and
angles. A girl
said my

dick is my best
quality. I took
it as a compliment,

but now I'm stretching
it out in the mirror,
keeping my face out

of the camera's frame,
and wondering why
no one is texting back.

WHICH MANSON?

With a beard
long as Charlie Manson's,
hiding my face well, but

I could feel spots with
thinner hair, or
not there. Lovers

told me it looked good,
but I could feel them
staring.

I shaved my whole head
thinking I was humbling
myself before God, but

God never said anything
nice about my face either.

OINK

My grandmother's friend,
pinched my stomach and called

me a little piggy. He had to
hold a handkerchief over
the hole in his neck to speak.

That's the day I stopped
looking in reflective
surfaces. That's the day

I knew
other people saw me,
and were disgusted.

LOCKED BATHROOM DOOR

Maybe there was
a thing needing
doing. I've hurt

many people with
my kicks for kicks.
Nothing more

embarrassing than
an angry child. One
time a kid pushed

me over a pile of
soccer balls. He said
he couldn't see me,

I was just another
round thing among
other round things.

After dinner, I ran
to the bathroom, and
pushed on my diaphragm

like it was a pump
that would get all this
shame out of my body.

PLAY

I got called fatty so much
it could have been my
legal name. No one

wanted to say they
were friend's with the
fat kid. I don't

say I love myself,
because even I don't want
to be seen with me.

TRICHTILLOMANIA

This friend pulls out
her hair. Not big I-
hate-you clumps, but

follicle by follicle. She
used to groom her cat
the same way. She feels

her body between
her fingers, looking
for something that

doesn't belong.

ONE BUSTED WHEEL

My father got
mad about us
revealing him.

Never smile, it lets
them know how
poor we are.

Stay out of people's
way in the aisles of
grocery stores. You

can't let them see
our cart full of instant
noodles
and have time to judge.

My shape became
partly what I ate,
partly the lies I told.

HANDS FOR MARTINIS AND A FACE FOR RADIO

There are too many
things wrong with my
fingers. I can only type

my self-loathing. I could
not play the song of my
disappointments

with a guitar, or draw
my Swiss cheese mind. My
hands

shake, and the digits
aretoostubby. I keep
them tucked away,

hidden from
the discriminations
of others. Someone I used

to love, we once shared a right
pocket, walking in the snow.

TAKE IT LYING DOWN

I blamed GOD for my appearance
up until I stopped believing in
anything. Then I blamed my

mother for lowering her standards.
It was all broken hearted beams
of light piercing my belly, overhanging

my belt. Never had many people
approach. Never been approachable,
but now I fly a white flag every time

I leave the house. White flags mean
peace, innocence, purity, but also
it shows that I surrender.

TOOTHLESS LYCANTHROPY

I felt
the fur
on my

arms.
My ears
were so

sensitive.
I heard
breaking

and
entering
with a

tail
between
my legs.

Had this
creeping
feeling

"I'm not
in the
right form."

Wanted
to be
a wolf,

but of course I
was just
A dog.

PINCH

She hunched over the mattress
without a frame, her neck craned to
the left picking tiny pieces

of skin from her arm. Picking with
her one long fingernail that she kept
for utility, she said. She hides her

arms with long sleeved red sweaters.
Rarely saw her wear white without
blood spots on the sleeves. Worst

of all, she's the one who
taught me that all my love
could change nothing.

KEEP THE CURLS

Used to spend
an hour with hands
gummy with hair gel

disappearing
my curls. Disappear
my genetics. All the

other kids had
perfectly straight hair.
and not fitting in

seemed like a crime.

AGING, MENTALLY ILL HIPSTER

Never thought age
crept out my window
like a raccoon of

youth. Glowing eyes in
the night, leering at
the chins on display.

The hitherto reactions
to my birthdate, wearing
skinny jeans to compensate.

No wrinkles yet, but that
damned flab of neck will
force me out the gene pool.

NIGHTLIGHT

Her body is always
covered by the night.
Not even the moon
is allowed into the
bedroom.

Always, "darling, turn
the light off
before I come to bed."

IT'S ART

She'd never tattoo
over her razor
scars, they were too

deep, and a form
of art
in their own way.

BRIDGE

Lumbering down the ogreish
sidewalk, sweating, dripping
On the concrete. I've been

stuck in my head afraid
to come out of the first
layer of protection a

person has outside the womb.
My body in pieces, a homunculus
of good intentions. It always breaks,

it's always too much strain. I was
used as a bridge over troubled
waters, until I became more

trouble than it was worth.

BARRIER

I don't remember my two parents
being in love. I can't remember
being in the same room as them

together, outside of one
Christmas. They were
always at opposite ends

of a car, screaming.
Couldn't figure
out a way to

wear my skin that would
keep them from hating
each other.

FAST FORWARD THE SEX SCENES

At first, sex was horrifying,
and being naked a rank sin. Next
it was hiding under the covers

and being undressed but not
seen. Also, I used to tweak—
giggling at any touch below

the neck. Now, it's all
muted. Sometimes I
leave my body behind

to be comforted,
as I float
through the window.

DING

My profile picture
is the only thing
on Facebook
with a dislike
button.

CHIMNEY

When I smoke
and walk
down the street,

people flee in
terror
escaping

the look of
angry disappointment
my face has.

LICENSE

It's an odd request:
"cover your eyes
before speaking to me."

My teeth are gnarled
and grey. Evidence
that I've stopped caring

I guess? Maybe it's true.
Maybe it's true that I'm not
supposed to end up with her.

GROWTH BEFORE WEALTH

I'm talking
to my date and
I feel a mole-hair
sprout from my cheek,
and I
stand up
and walk out
never to be seen again.

INTERLUDE

Do not read any
further.

Nothing good
will come
of
it.

(I'm serious)

BLISTER PACKED

Society captures us when
we're young. Either a
Barbie or superhero
action movie star.

Corporate BDSM, two
roles: You're either
Dom or sub, and

good parents want
their children to be
neither. No wonder

the best ones come
out a little warped.
a little broken, missing

arms, legs or missiles.
growing up is hard,
harder still when you

29

do it in a box.

TOUGH

Repetitive. It's
repetitive to wake up

everyday in the
same body while

wishing you could
be an 80% improved

version of yourself.
I've prayed for less

and more. A brain
resilient as

lizard skin

to neglect, or perhaps
a better appetite

for food.

EAR BUDDIES

There is a preference
to exist in only black
and white.

There is a preference
to bow your head around
people.

There is a preference
to move a mood up and down
to the beat of music only
you can hear.

PUNITIVE MEASURES

We were in the car
in Washington, Mt. Baker
ahead or behind us, and

my grandmother kept
slapping my hand

telling me
"don't touch your face."

CAUSE MEDIC SURGERY

"She got
a lip
implant. Can you
BELIEVE she would
ever do a thing?
She is prettier
than she thinks she is."

"Maybe you should tell her someday,"

ASKING THE TOUGH QUESTIONS

My face sagged in the mirror, so much
that I got both ears pierced.

It was supposed to add symmetry
to my face. Instead, my friend's

french mother asked me,
"ARE YOU FAG?"

A BROKEN EXERCISE BICYCLE

The machine creaking
of a stair master filling the
closing gym, trying to conquer

my body's detestation, and
escaping the bubble of

rejection I was trapped in.
It was much healthier than

other things I could
have done.

THE UNSEEN

My body exists at the
edge of personhood,

I am not here to
have a good time

I'm here existing
outside your periphery

like a caterer
you never hired.

9 781798 121399